OCEAN DIVERS

Anita Ganeri

Chicago, Illinois

www.heinemannraintree.com
Visit our website to find out
more information about
Heinemann-Raintree books.

To order:
☎ Phone 888-454-2279
🖥 Visit www.heinemannraintree.com
to browse our catalog and order online.

Edited by Rebecca Rissman, Dan Nunn,
    and Sian Smith
Designed by Joanna Hinton Malivoire
Picture research by Elizabeth Alexander
Production by Victoria Fitzgerald
Originated by Capstone Global Library
Printed and bound in China by CTPS

15 14 13 12 11
10 9 8 7 6 5 4 3 2 1

**Library of Congress Cataloging-in-Publication
Data**
Ganeri, Anita, 1961-
  Ocean divers / Anita Ganeri.
    p. cm.—(Landform adventurers)
  Includes bibliographical references and index.
  ISBN 978-1-4109-4140-4 (hb)—ISBN 978-1-4109-4147-
3 (pb) 1. Oceanographers—Juvenile literature. 2. Divers—
Juvenile literature. I. Title.
  GC30.5.G36 2012
  551.46092—dc22   2010050063

Acknowledgments
We would like to thank the following for permission
to reproduce photographs: Corbis pp. 5 (© Michele
Westmorland/Science Faction), 9 (© Gary Bell), 13 (©
NASA), 14 (© Jeffrey L. Rotman), 20 (© Norbert Wu/
Science Faction), 22 (© Jeffrey L. Rotman), 24 (© Ralph
White), 25 (© Julian Calverley), 26 (© Julie Dermansky);
Getty Images pp. 10 (Steve Mason/Photodisc), 18 (Ira
Block/National Geographic); © Image Quest Marine p.
17; Photo by Advanced Imaging & Visulization Lab p. 21
(©Woods Hole Oceanographic Institution); Photolibrary
pp. 7 (Purestock), 11 (imagebroker), 27 (Enrico Sacchetti);
Science Photo Library pp. 6 (Alexis Rosenfeld), 12
(Martin Jakobsson), 15 (Klein Associates), 16 (Georgette
Douwma), 19 (Alexis Rosenfeld), 28 (Simon Fraser),
29 (Matthew Oldfield); Shutterstock pp. 4 (© Map
Resources), 8 (© Specta), 23 (© Brandelet).

Cover photograph of Caribbean reef sharks reproduced
with permission of Photolibrary (David B Fleetham/OSF).

Every effort has been made to contact copyright holders
of material reproduced in this book. Any omissions will
be rectified in subsequent printings if notice is given to
the publisher.

Disclaimer
All the Internet addresses (URLs) given in this book were
valid at the time of going to press. However, due to the
dynamic nature of the Internet, some addresses may
have changed, or sites may have changed or ceased to
exist since publication. While the author and publisher
regret any inconvenience this may cause readers, no
responsibility for any such changes can be accepted by
either the author or the publisher.

Some words are shown in bold, **like this**. You can find
out what they mean by looking in the glossary.

Contents

What Are Oceans?

Oceans are huge stretches of salty water. They cover about two-thirds of Earth. There are five oceans: the Pacific, Atlantic, Indian, Southern, and Arctic.

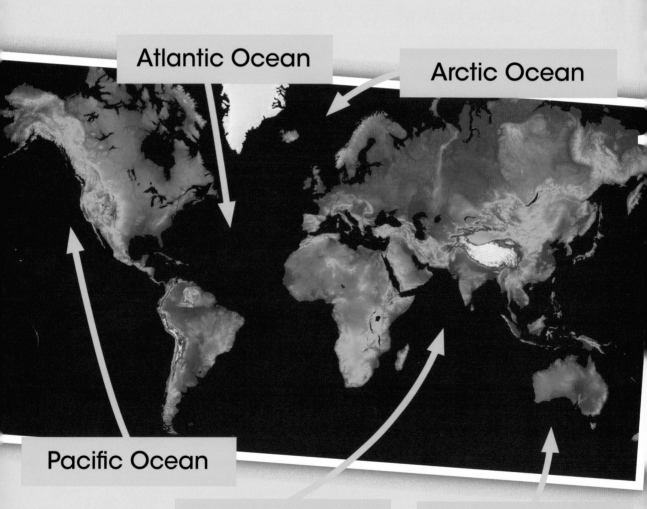

Atlantic Ocean

Arctic Ocean

Pacific Ocean

Indian Ocean

Southern Ocean

From colorful coral reefs to the dark,
deep sea, oceans are amazing places
for scientists to explore. Are you ready
to dive in?

Exploring the Oceans

Scientists who study the oceans are called **oceanographers**. They look at sea plants and animals, underwater geography, such as volcanoes, and sunken shipwrecks.

Oceanographers have lots of ways to study the oceans. They use ships with special **instruments**, computers, **submersibles**, and even **satellites** in outer space.

OCEAN FACT
Satellites look at waves, sea temperature, and ocean **pollution**.

Remarkable Reefs

Where can you see fish that look like butterflies, starfish, and giant clams? The answer is on a coral reef. The Great Barrier Reef in Australia is so big that it can be seen from space!

Huge coral reefs grow in warm oceans.

OCEAN FACT
Coral reefs are built
by tiny animals, called
coral polyps.

Ocean Diving

Marine biologists dive underwater to look at life on a coral reef. They have to wear special **scuba diving** suits. They carry tanks of air on their backs to breathe. They may also carry underwater cameras to take photos of the creatures they see.

fin

OCEAN FACT
Divers wear flipper-like fins on their feet to help them swim.

Seabed Features

You might think the seabed is flat. But it has mountains, valleys, and volcanoes, just like the land! The Mid-Atlantic Ridge is a chain of mountains in the Atlantic Ocean. It is about 10,000 miles long. That is about 12 times the length of California!

Mid-Atlantic Ridge

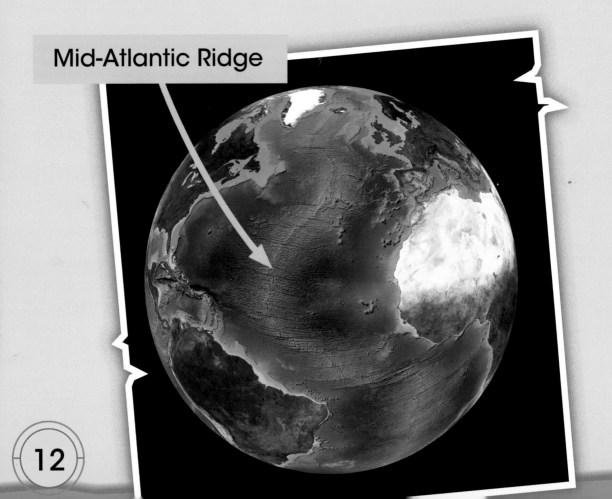

Maui, Hawaii

OCEAN FACT
The islands of Hawaii are the tops of underwater volcanoes.

Using Sound

Scientists have special **instruments** that use sound to make maps of the seabed, showing what it looks like. They are called **sonar** instruments. Ships on the surface pull the instruments across the seabed.

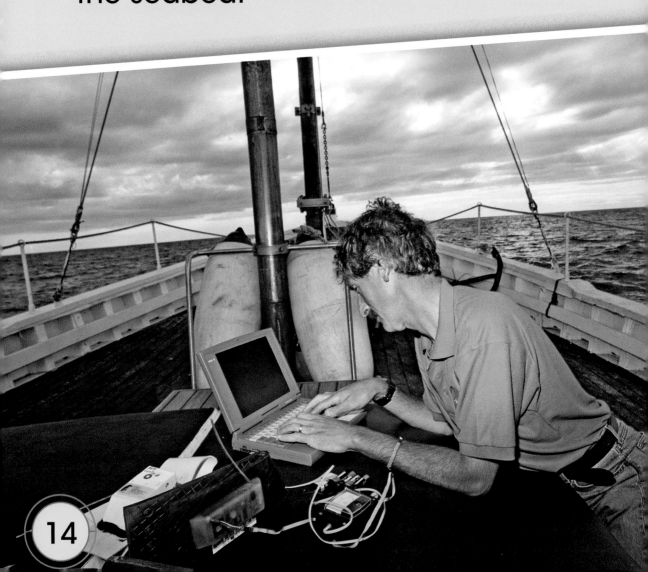

OCEAN FACT
Sonar can even be used to find underwater shipwrecks!

shipwreck

Atlantic Ocean, off Massachusetts

15

Fiery Fountains

In 1977 scientists saw fountains of hot water gushing up from **vents** in the seabed. They also found giant tube worms and other extraordinary animals living around the vents.

vent

OCEAN FACT
Giant tube worms can grow to about 10 feet long. That's taller than a person!

17

Mini Submarines

Scientists travel in mini submarines called **submersibles** to explore the deep sea. It is cramped and cold inside a submersible. But it is exciting to look out the windows as it sinks deeper and deeper.

submersible

OCEAN FACT
It can take a submersible about three hours to dive 13,000 feet.

Roving Robots

A **trench** is a deep dip in the ocean floor. It can be dangerous for scientists to dive into trenches. Instead, they send robots called ROVs (Remote-Operated Vehicles). Scientists on board a ship work the ROVs. The ROVs have lights and cameras for taking pictures.

OCEAN FACT
In 2009 an ROV called *Nereus* dived to the bottom of the Mariana Trench, the deepest place on Earth.

Studying Wildlife

Scientists who study ocean wildlife are called **marine biologists**. One of their jobs is to tag sharks. First, they track the shark by boat. Then, they fix a tag to its back fin. By following the tagged sharks, scientists can learn more about where they swim.

shark

whale shark

OCEAN FACT

The biggest fish in the sea is the whale shark. It can grow 60 feet long. That is about the length of 1½ school buses!

Shipwreck!

In 1985 an ROV called *Argo* found the wreck of the *Titanic*. The *Titanic* was a famous ship that sank in 1912, when it hit an iceberg.

Argo

OCEAN FACT

Marine archaeologists look for shipwrecks and sunken cities under the sea. Sometimes they even find long-lost pirate treasure.

Oil Spill

In April 2010 an oil rig exploded in the Gulf of Mexico. Huge amounts of oil spilled into the sea. This led to **pollution** on the shore, and it killed wildlife. Scientists used planes and **satellites** to check how the oil spread. Ships sucked up some of the oil.

ROV controls

OCEAN FACT
ROVs were sent down into the sea to try to fix the leaking pipe.

Becoming an Oceanographer

If you want to be an **oceanographer**, you need to be good at science. You may also need to study a subject such as **marine biology** in college.

Being an oceanographer is an exciting career. You might be based in a laboratory on land for some of the time. But you may also get to travel to oceans all over the world!

Glossary

coral polyps tiny sea creatures, related to jellyfish, that build coral reefs

instrument equipment used by scientists

marine archaeologist scientist who studies ancient ruins and objects found in the sea

marine biologist scientist who studies living things in the sea

marine biology study of living things in the sea

oceanographer scientist who studies oceans

pollution making the sea dirty by dumping chemicals, trash, or oil into it

satellite device in space that travels around Earth and collects information

scuba diving diving in a wetsuit with an aqualung (tank of air) on the back

sonar instrument that uses sound to make maps of the seabed

submersible vehicle like a mini submarine, used for exploring the deep sea

trench deep valley under the sea

vent opening in Earth's crust from which gases escape

Find Out More

Find out

Where is the deepest point in the ocean?

Books

Claybourne, Anna. *100 Things You Should Know About Extreme Earth*. Broomall, Pa.: Mason Crest, 2009.

Morrison, Marianne. *Mysteries of the Sea: How Divers Explore the Ocean.* Washington, D.C.: National Geographic, 2006.

Woodward, John. *Oceans Atlas with CD-ROM*. New York: Dorling Kindersley, 2007.

Websites

http://kids.earth.nasa.gov/archive/career/oceanographer.html
Discover if a career as an oceanographer or marine biologist is right for you.

http://oceanservice.noaa.gov/kids
Find out lots of information and amazing facts from the National Oceanic and Atmospheric Administration (NOAA) kids' site.

Index